DID YOU KNOW?

RAiNBOWS NEVER END

and other fun facts

For Alex
—L. D.

For Ethan and Theo
—H. E.

For Sam
—P. O.

LITTLE SIMON
An imprint of Simon & Schuster Children's Publishing Division
1230 Avenue of the Americas, New York, New York 10020
Series concept by Laura Lyn DiSiena
Copyright © 2014 by Simon & Schuster, Inc.
For information about special discounts for bulk purchases, please contact Simon & Schuster Special Sales at 1-866-506-1949 or business@simonandschuster.com.
The Simon & Schuster Speakers Bureau can bring authors to your live event. For more information or to book an event contact the
Simon & Schuster Speakers Bureau at 1-866-248-3049 or visit our website at www.simonspeakers.com.
Manufactured in China 1018 SCP
10 9 8 7 6 5 4 3
Library of Congress Cataloging-in-Publication Data
DiSiena, Laura Lyn, author.
Rainbows never end : and other fun facts / by Laura Lyn DiSiena and Hannah Eliot ;
illustrated by Pete Oswald. — First edition. pages cm. — (Did you know?)
1. Rainbows--Juvenile literature. 2. Meteorology—Miscellanea—Juvenile literature.
3. Science—Miscellanea—Juvenile literature. 4. Children's questions and answers.
I. Eliot, Hannah, author. II. Oswald, Pete, illustrator. III. Title.
QC976.R2D57 2014   551.502—dc23   2013049947
ISBN 978-1-4814-0275-0 (pbk)
ISBN 978-1-4814-0277-4 (hc)
ISBN 978-1-4814-0278-1 (eBook)

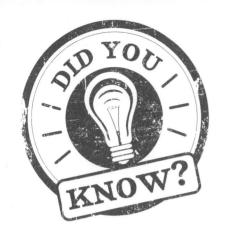
DID YOU KNOW?

RAINBOWS NEVER END

and other fun facts

By Laura Lyn DiSiena and Hannah Eliot
Illustrated by Pete Oswald

LITTLE SIMON
New York   London   Toronto   Sydney   New Delhi

HELLO THERE!

Have you ever seen a rainbow? It was probably raining, or had just stopped raining, right?

Did you know that rainbows appear when sunlight hits drops of water at *just* the right angle? How about that no two people see the same rainbow? And that all rainbows are made up of seven colors— red, orange, yellow, green, blue, indigo, and violet?
Okay, so you did know those things. But did you know that rainbows NEVER END?

THAT'S RIGHT!

Although rainbows appear to
be arcs, they're actually full circles.
The reason we usually only see an arc
is because the horizon of the Earth blocks
us from seeing the rest. The only way you'd
be able to see the full circle of a rainbow is if
you were up in the sky looking down onto it.
And because rainbows are circles, that means
they don't have an end point. They just
keep going around and around . . .
and around and around . . . and . . .
well, you get the point.

HOT! HOT! HOT!

So now you know that the sun helps to create rainbows, and that rainbows never end, but did you know that the sun is a star? At the center of our solar system, it's the star closest to Earth. But it's still about 92,960,000 miles away! It takes around 8 minutes for the sun's light to travel that distance and reach Earth.

Not only does the sun give off its own light, it also gives light to the moon. The moon reflects this light from the sun—and that's why the moon glows!

Snow is also a big reflector of sunlight. For this reason,
it's important to wear sunscreen, even in the wintertime!

Snow is created when the temperature drops below freezing and crystals form in the clouds. The crystals fall through the clouds, bumping into one another along the way, creating unique and complex snowflake designs! All snowflakes have six sides, but NO TWO snowflakes are exactly the same.

Snowflakes usually fall pretty slowly from the sky—at just 3 miles per hour. Raindrops, on the other hand, fall much faster—at about 18 miles per hour. And raindrops are not actually tear-drop shaped like they are often depicted. They're round!

Did you know you can predict rain by looking at a pinecone? That's right! A pinecone's scales will close if rain is on the way.

And did you know that rain is *recycled* water? It's water from Earth's lakes, rivers, oceans, and seas that has evaporated up into the clouds. That evaporated water then falls from the clouds in different forms of precipitation—such as rain and snow.

New clouds are constantly forming. It can take anywhere from a few minutes to 1 hour for a cloud to form. They can grow vertically or horizontally, and they can also be different shapes! Have you ever seen funny shapes in the clouds?

A cumulonimbus cloud forms close to the ground and can grow vertically to be 5 miles high or more. This is the type of cloud that forms during thunderstorms.

Did you know that about 1,800 thunderstorms occur on Earth each day?

That's a lot of thunder! Something else that often occurs during thunderstorms is lightning. In fact, thunder is actually the sound *caused* by lightning. Lightning is a powerful burst of electricity that happens very quickly during a storm. Lightning heats up the air around it to as much as 50,000 degrees Fahrenheit! That's 5 times hotter than the surface of the sun!

Thunderstorms sometimes turn into tornadoes. A tornado is a spinning windstorm that creates a tunnel of air that touches both the ground and a cloud. Extreme tornadoes can reach wind speeds of more than 300 miles per hour. But a tornado typically only lasts a few minutes—that's not long at all!

Have you heard of the summer solstice? In the northern hemisphere, it usually occurs on June 21 each year, because that's when the northern hemisphere is most tilted toward the sun. During the summer solstice, there are 24 hours of SUNLiGHT at the North Pole . . .

and 24 hours of DARKNESS at the South Pole!

What *is* the North Pole, anyway? A pole in the middle of the snow? A bunch of igloos? Well, the North Pole *isn't* a piece of land. It's actually a floating sheet of ice in a place called the Arctic Circle. In the winter, the ice grows to be as big as the United States of America. In the summer, the ice melts to half that size!

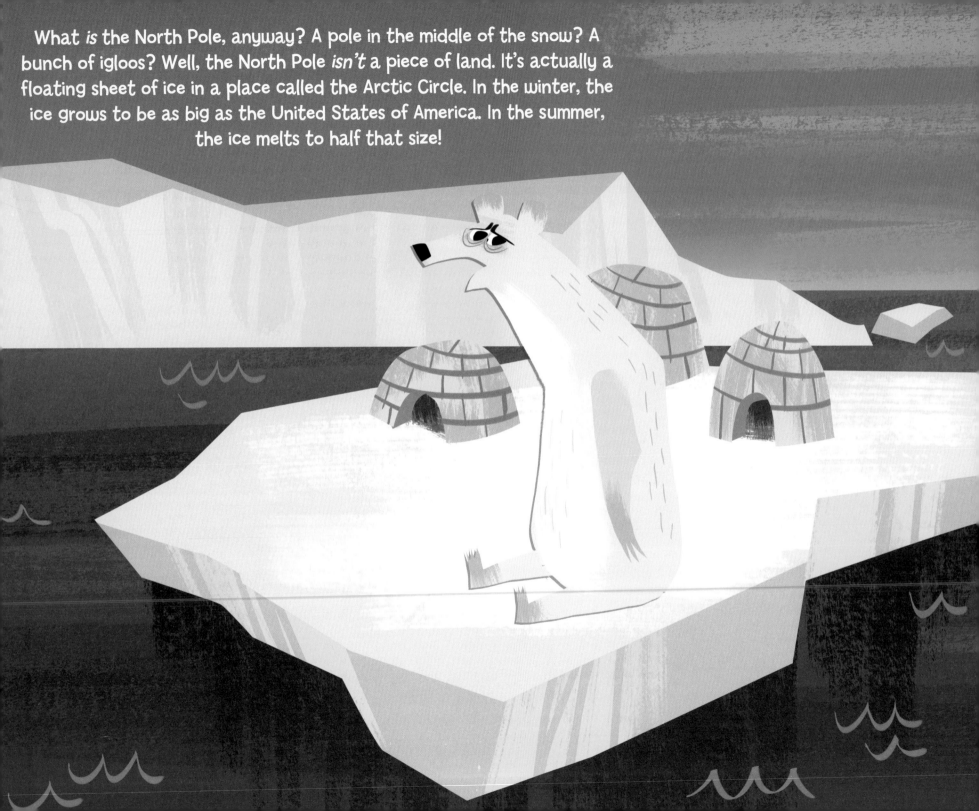

Speaking of ice in the Arctic, did you know that flowers can be found in the middle of the Arctic Ocean? They're called frost flowers. Frost flowers form when the air above the ice becomes saturated with moisture. The frost flowers grow as they pick up salt and marine bacteria in the air, forming flower-like structures!

The South Pole is a sheet of ice as well, but it's on land that's also known as Antarctica. Even though Antarctica is incredibly cold . . . it's actually a desert! That's because deserts are places that get fewer than 10 inches of rainfall all year. Can you imagine? That's only about 2 tall glasses of water!

Usually, though, deserts are pretty hot. And as you might guess, the hottest place on Earth is a desert. It's Death Valley, California, where the highest temperature ever recorded was 134 degrees Fahrenheit!

Another cool thing about Death Valley is that the rocks there can fly.
WAIT—ROCKS CAN FLY?
Scientists still haven't figured out how, but in Death Valley, boulders
that weigh up to 700 pounds will sometimes go sliding across flat
land, leaving trails behind them. A rock will move anywhere from
a few inches to nearly 3,000 feet!

Deserts are the driest parts of the planet. Rain forests, on the other hand, are areas near the equator that are very humid and warm. There, rain falls more than 90 days a year. That's 3 months of straight rain if you put it all together! Rain forests have some of the most interesting wildlife. There are butterflies, jaguars, snakes, and plenty of fruits and plants, too.

A lot of the food we eat originally came from a rain forest. Think about it—chocolate, potatoes, corn, bananas . . . and much more. *Yum!*

You can probably guess by now that with all that rain, there are plenty of rainbows in a rain forest! But you might not have heard of a very rare rainbow that can only be seen by the light of a full moon. It's called a MOONBOW.
The Victoria Falls rain forest is one of the few places on Earth where a moonbow can be seen regularly.

Rainbows and moonbows aren't the only things
that make beautiful colors in the sky.
An aurora is a display of colored lights that
ripple, glow, and swirl across the night sky!
An aurora occurs when millions of tiny particles
fly from the sun into space at supersonic speed!
Those particles are powered by solar
wind—a type of wind that occurs only in space.

You see, just like here on Earth,
there's wind out there in the universe.
And just like rainbows, the universe NEVER ENDS!

MORE FUN FACTS

Sun: The sun is so big that Earth could fit inside it a million times!

Rainbow: A supernumerary rainbow is one that has several faint rainbows on the inner side of the main rainbow.

Snow: Watermelon snow is snow that has algae growing on it. The algae is reddish-pink in color—like a watermelon!

Moon: Neil Armstrong was the first person to step on the moon. He did this on July 21, 1969.

Clouds: Clouds are not always white. They can be gray during thunderstorms, and red, orange, and pink at sunset. There is even something called *cloud iridescence*. When small water droplets in the clouds scatter light, the clouds will contain many different colors all at once!

Tornado: There are other types of windstorms that aren't tornadoes, such as dust devils, fire whirls, and steam devils.

Rain: The umbrella wasn't invented to protect people from the rain—it was to protect them from the sun! Some people still use umbrellas in this way.

North Pole: At the North Pole, all directions point south!

Thunder: Even though thunder is the sound caused by lightning, light travels faster than sound, so we see lightning first!

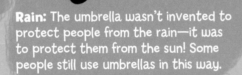

Antarctica: There are no permanent residents of Antarctica—meaning that not a single person lives there year-round.

Moonbow: Moonbows are fainter than rainbows because there is a smaller amount of light reflected from the surface of the moon.

Rain forest: They may cover less than 2 percent of the Earth's total surface area, but rain forests are home to 50 percent of the Earth's plants and animals.

Desert: The animals that live in deserts are used to environments with very little water. The kangaroo rat never even needs to drink water—it gets everything it needs from the seeds it eats!

BANG!

Universe: The big bang theory is a theory that the universe was created when a big bang occurred 10 to 20 billion years ago. After that, the matter that already existed began forming into individual planets and stars . . . and the rest is theoretical history!

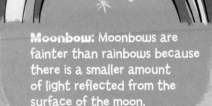